Are We There Yet?
All About the Planet Neptune!
Space for Kids
Children's Aeronautics & Space Book

BABY PROFESSOR

EDUCATION KIDS

Neptune is the eighth planet from the Sun.

Neptune is a large blue planet with a hydrogen-methane atmosphere and faint rings.

Neptune is nearly four times larger than the Earth.

It is also the fourth largest planet in our solar system.

Neptune experiences the most violent weather among all planets in the Solar System.

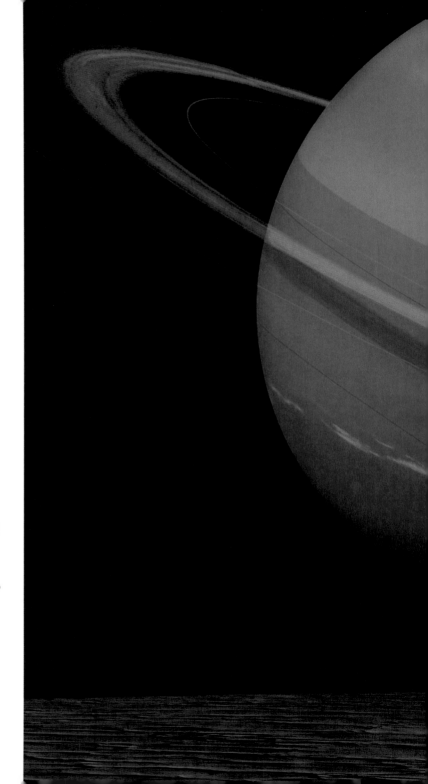

Storms have been seen swirling around its surface.

Neptune is covered with white clouds that are spread out around the planet.

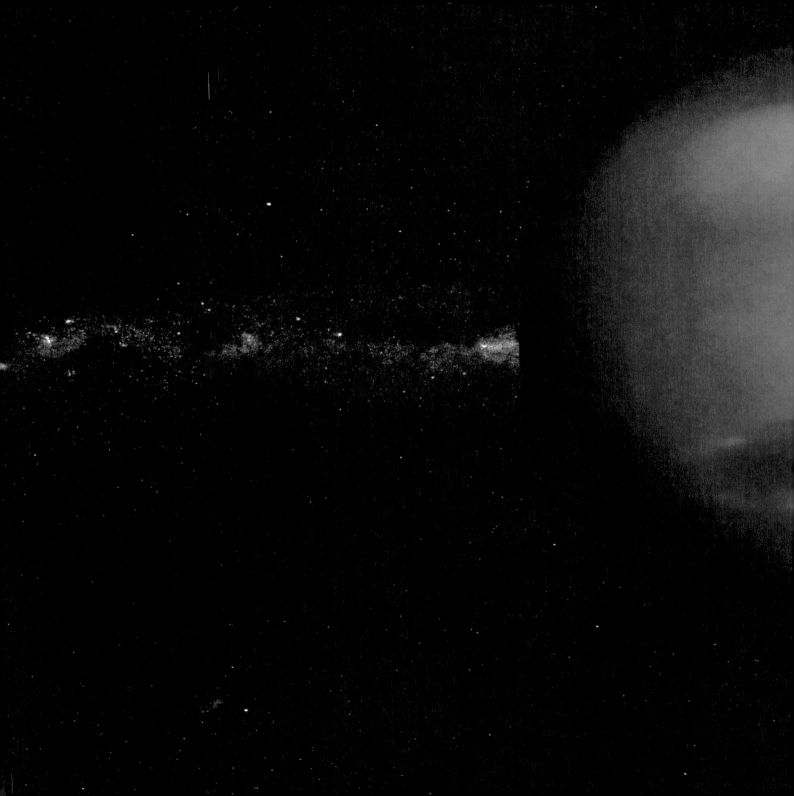

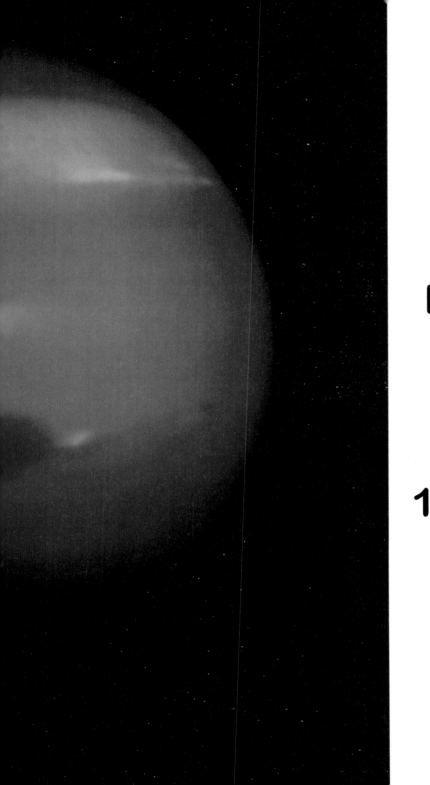

Neptune was first seen through a telescope in 1846 in Berlin.

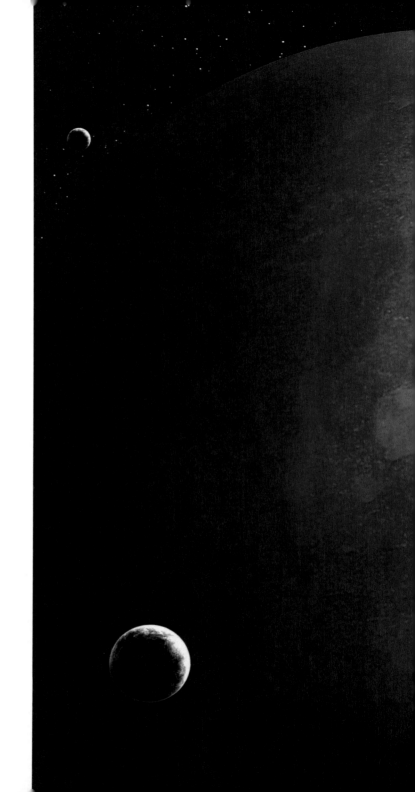

Neptune is a large ball of hydrogen and helium.

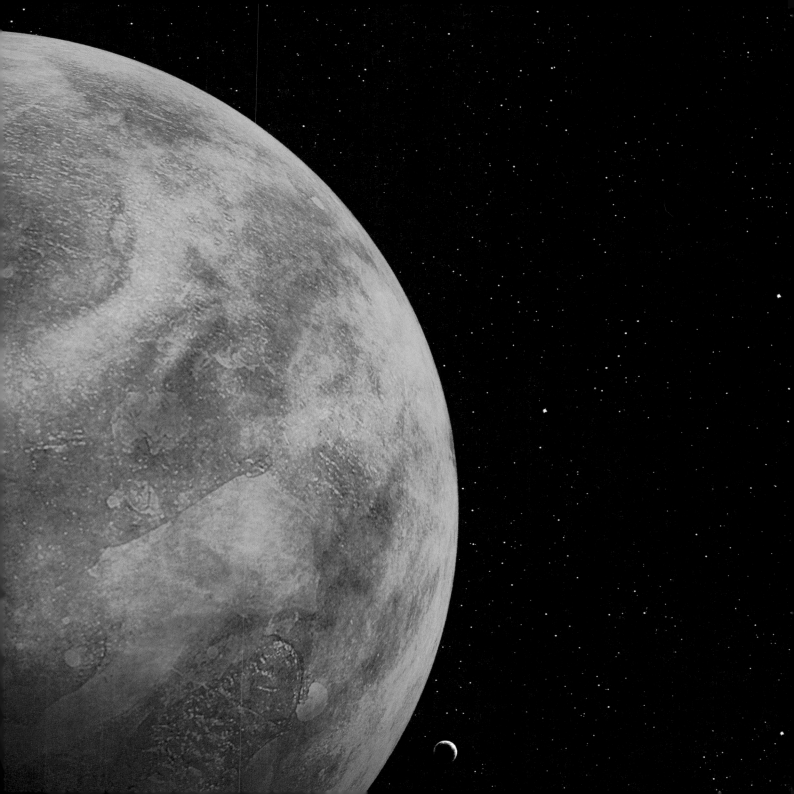

Therefore,
there are no
rocky surfaces
to walk on.

Neptune takes 165 Earth years to orbit the Sun.

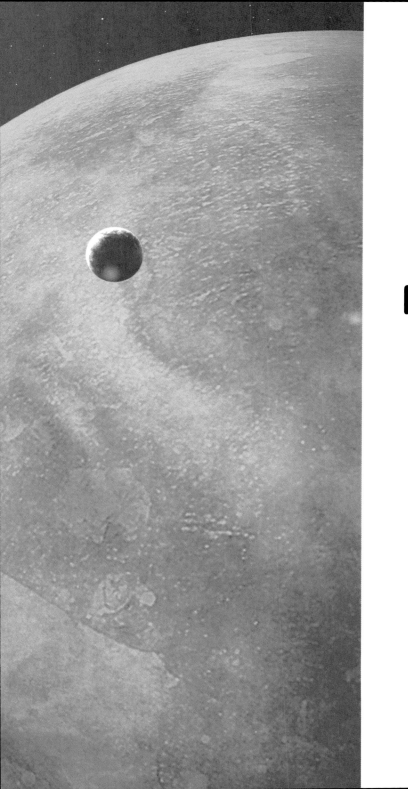

Neptune takes
just over 19
hours to turn
around on
its axis.

Neptune is 2,793 million miles away from the Sun.

In 1846,
its first
moon was
discovered—
Triton.

Triton orbits in an opposite direction to the rest of Neptune's moons.

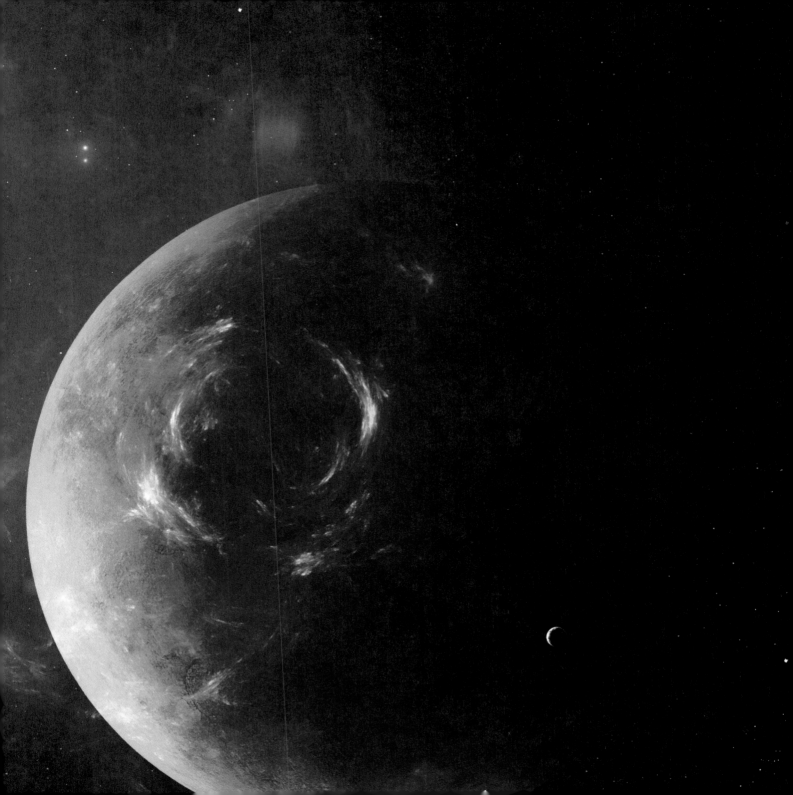

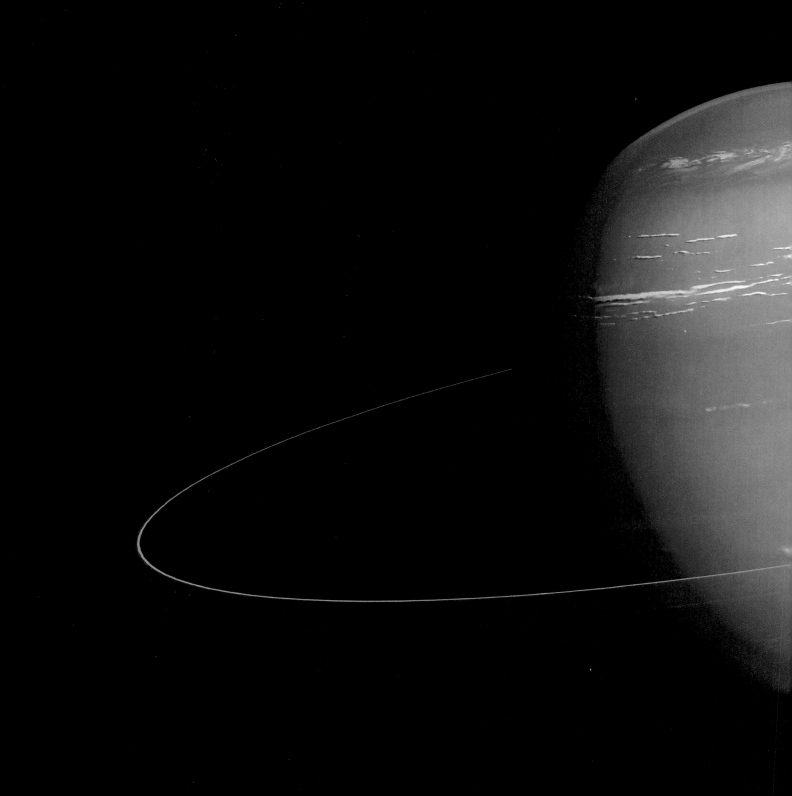

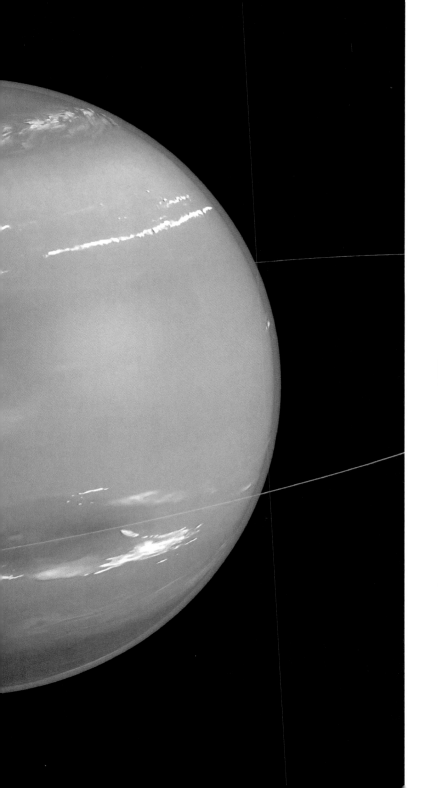

Today,
Neptune has
13 known
moons.

Neptune is the coldest planet in the Solar System.

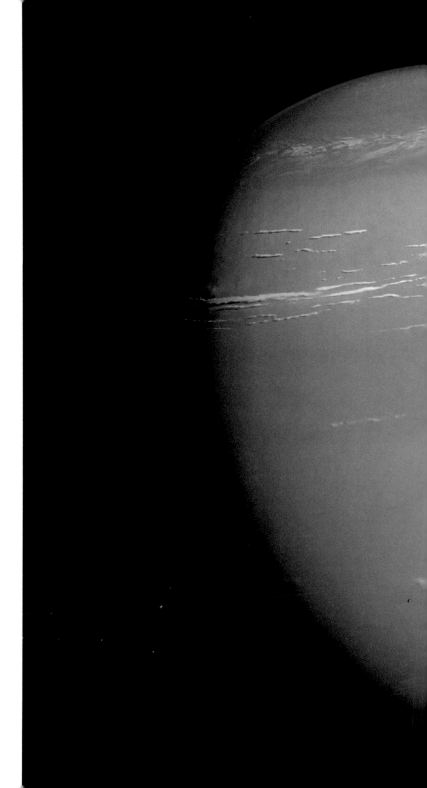

Neptune was the first planet discovered by mathematical calculation.

Research and learn more about the planet NEPTUNE! Have fun!

Made in the USA
Middletown, DE
08 September 2020